NATIONAL GEOGRAPHIC

School Publishing

T0042391

What's the Matter?

PIONEER EDITION

By Barbara Keeler

CONTENTS

What's the Matter?

When you think of the beach, do you think of plastic? Probably not! But plastic is a type of matter, and matter is everywhere. Even at the beach! Bathing suits are made with plastic fibers. Surfboards have plastic parts. Coolers are made with plastic. You can find plastic almost everywhere.

Making Plastic

Plastic is made with materials found in nature. Most plastic is made from fossil fuels. Oil, natural gas, and coal are **fossil fuels.** Fossil fuels are made up of the changed remains of things that lived long ago.

Scientists can change the properties of plastic so it can do different jobs. They can make it become tough or soft. The texture can change.

Part of Plastic. Oil is a fossil fuel that is used to make plastic.

Shaping Plastic

Plastic is heated to make different shapes. When it melts, it is put into a mold. The liquid plastic takes the shape of the mold. Then it cools and hardens into a solid.

Have you used a plastic foam cup? Think about how it felt. Sometimes tiny gas bubbles are added to liquid plastic. This makes the plastic foamy.

You can shape warm plastic. To make plastic tubes, the plastic is squeezed out. To make plastic wrap, plastic is rolled out in long sheets.

Hot Stuff. This plastic is going through heated rollers to become solid, flexible sheets.

Keeping Cool. Plastic foam is good for insulation.

Using Plastic

Plastic is in a lot of things. Think about clothing and carpet. Plastic is used to make them. Do you want clothes that don't shrink or wrinkle? Try nylon and polyester. They are fabrics made of plastic fibers. Have you touched the handle of a hot pan? Most aren't hot. That's because plastic is good for **insulation**. Insulation stops the flow of heat.

Plastic is often used for parts of cars, buses, and planes. It is strong and light.

These are just a few things that you use every day that are made with plastic.

Preventing Burns. These plastic handles do not melt.

Lighten Up. Many parts of a car are made of plastic. It is lighter than metal.

Types of Plastic

Most plastic is made with one of seven types of plastic. The numbers on the plastic tell you what type it is and if it is safe to use with heat.

1 PETE Clear, cheap, tough. Used in carpet, drink bottles, other things

Five two-liter #1 bottles can be recycled to make an extra large T-shirt.

2 HDPE Stiff, strong. Used in shampoo and milk bottles, other things

3 V Lightweight, tough. Used in window frames, fences, CDs, other things

4 LDPE Tough, flexible. Toys, lids, squeeze bottles, other things

5 PP Doesn't melt easily. Used to hold hot foods and drinks, other things

6 PS Often made into plastic foam. Used in packing peanuts, food and drink containers, other things

7 OTHER Mix of plastics. Used in mixed plastic containers or products

Problems with Plastics

Plastic can be useful. But it can also cause problems. Plastic is made from dangerous chemicals, or **toxins**. These can get into food and drinks. They can hurt people. Be sure to use plastic containers that are safe for hot things. Look for plastic marked with #5 or #6.

Plastic also uses up resources. Oil is used to make plastic. Oil is limited. We use it faster than it forms.

Most plastic is not recycled. Most recycling centers will not accept all types of plastic. So plastic can make a lot of trash.

Plastic stays around for a long time. It does not break down easily. After a very long time, plastic may break into tiny pieces. These pieces of plastic pollute Earth. They can even hurt animals.

Trapped. This bird has plastic stuck around its beak.

What You Can Do

How can you use less plastic? Take your own shopping bags to the store. Use a stainless steel water bottle instead of a plastic one.

When you buy something in a plastic container, look at the number on it. Be sure it can be recycled. This is called precycling!

Plastic makes life easier and better. But we shouldn't use more of it than we need.

Wordwise

fossil fuels: fuels that formed from the remains of things that lived millions of years ago

insulation: something that stops or slows the transfer of heat

toxins: dangerous chemicals

Steel: A Strong Mixture

Strong Connection. This bridge in New York is made of steel.

What Is Steel?

Steel is a very strong metal. It is made of iron and a little carbon. Iron is a strong metal. But if you mix it with carbon it becomes even stronger.

Why Is Steel Important?

Steel is used to make many things. Most cars and trucks have parts made of steel. Bridges, buildings, and ocean ships all contain steel. Steel makes all these objects strong and safe.

Making Steel

How do you make steel? Mix iron and a little bit of carbon. They are solids. To make steel, the solids must be melted into liquids. At high temperatures, the solids melt. They become a thick, gooey liquid. The iron and carbon mix and become a solution. Then the solution is rolled into sheets or put into molds. As the steel cools, it becomes hard and solid.

iron ore

carbon

These two materials mixed together become steel.

Iron melts when it is heated to high temperatures in this huge furnace.

steel beams for building

steel bolts

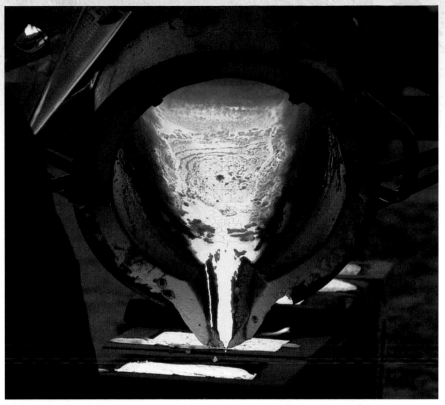

The liquid steel takes the shape of the mold.

steel tools

The process ends with a product.
These are just a few of the products
that are made from steel.

Steel is one of the world's most recycled
materials. About 68 percent of all steel
is recycled.

Properties of Matter

Find out what you have learned about the properties of plastics and steel.

1 How do we get most plastic?

2 What natural materials are used to make plastic?

3 Why is it important to know what type of plastic is used in a container?

4 What are some reasons to use less plastic?

5 How are steel and plastic different?